A Pilates Workout for Children

A Pilates Workout for Children

KATE HAWKINS

For more information,
email: pilatesforlifewithkate@gmail.com

FIRST EDITION

978-1-80227-659-6 (eBook)
978-1-80227-658-9 (paperback)

Dedicated to Pathways.

Thank you to Joan, Natasha,
Rob and my family.

What is your favourite animal?

How are you feeling today?

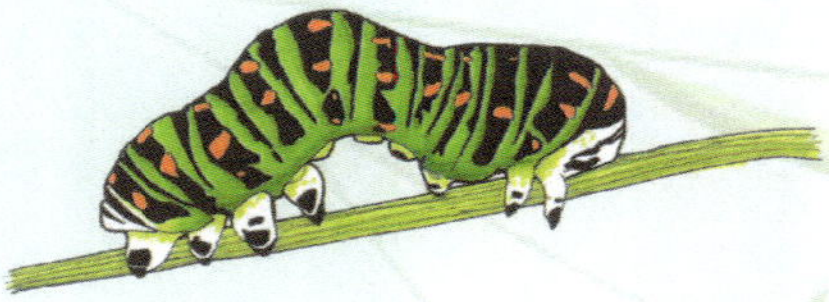

CALM

FEELING OK

HAPPY

SAD

LONELY

UNWELL

NERVOUS

WORRIED

EMBARRASSED

DISTRACTED

BORED

SILLY

FRUSTRATED

CROSS

ANGRY

**Time for some stretching,
swaying, leaning, reaching, jumping,
bending, balancing and breathing
to make us feel strong and calm.**

Breathe like a Panda

Sit with crossed legs. Palms on knees.
Close your eyes and breathe in through your nose
and out through your mouth.

Give yourself a hug like a Monkey

Stretch your arms out wide looking up and
then wrap them around your middle looking down.

Flap like a Butterfly

Sit with arms behind,
bring soles of feet together and
move your knees up and down.

Arch your back like a Cat

Put your hands and knees on the floor,
round your back and look at
your knees.

Roar like a Lion

Put your hands and knees on the floor.
Lift up your head, make a dip
in your back and roar!

Stretch like a Dog

Put your hands and feet on the floor
and lift your hips in the air.
Pedal your feet up and down.

Roll like a Hedgehog

Bring your knees into your chest and
wrap your hands around your knees.
Roll backwards and forwards.

Jump like a Frog

Squat down with your hands and feet on the floor.
Use your legs to jump up in the air.

Stretch like a Starfish

Stand with your legs and arms wide apart.
Stretch as high as you can. Spread out
your fingers and stand on tiptoe.

Lean like a Giraffe

Reach your arms up above your head
and bring your hands together.
Lean from side to side.

Sway like an Elephant

Stand with your feet wide, clasp your hands together in front and lower your body down. Sway from side to side.

Balance like a Flamingo

Stand on one leg and raise your knee.
Open your arms wide. Then swap feet.

Round down like a Penguin

Drop your head and roll down towards your feet looking at your knees then slowly roll all the way back up.

Be strong like a Horse

Put your hands and knees on the floor and stretch out one arm and the opposite leg. Then swap sides.

Crawl like a Bear

Put your hands and knees on the floor.
Flip your toes forwards and lift your knees up.
Crawl on your hands and toes forwards and backwards.

Hold still like a Crocodile

Put hands and knees on the floor, lift your knees and straighten your legs into one long line.

Hum like a Bee

Sit with crossed legs and hands behind your head.
Hum while rotating your body one way then the other.

Walk like a Crab

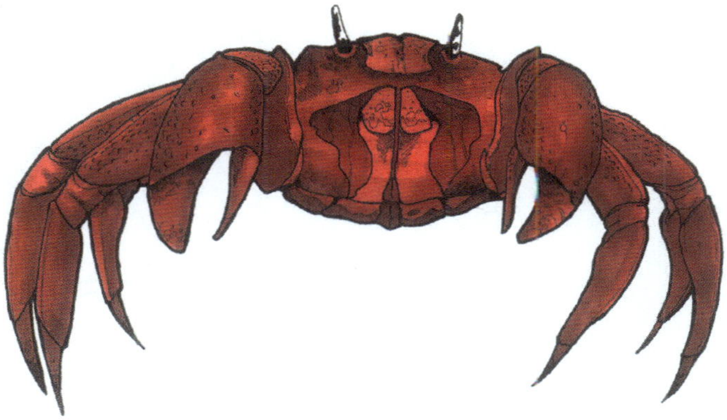

Sit feet on the floor, knees bent, arms behind and palms down, facing in. Lift hips in the air and move from side to side.

Clap like a Seal

Soles together, hands on ankles, lift feet up and balance.
Clap feet together 3 times, roll back and forwards.

Curl up like a Caterpillar

Lie down and roll up towards your toes.
Reach over looking at your knees and
then roll slowly all the way back.

Gallop like a Zebra

Lie on your back and lift your legs and arms in the air. Cycle your legs and arms round and round.

Slither like a Snake

Lie on your side in one long line. Rest your head on your arm and place your top arm on your top leg. Lift head and feet off the floor. Then swap sides.

Look up like a Swan

Lie face down, hands by your shoulders. Gently push onto your hands, straighten your arms and lift your chest.

Swim like a Fish

Lie face down with arms stretched forwards.
Lift arms and legs off the floor and
move them up and down.

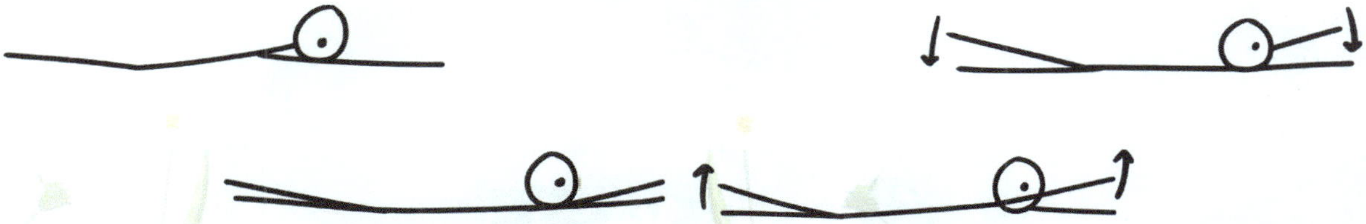

Hide like a Tortoise

Sit on your heels and curl over into a ball, head down looking at your knees. Relax your arms by your side. Breathe in through your nose and out through your mouth.

Well done!

Animals Move is finished!

Shake every part of your body,
smile and give yourself a clap.

What is your favourite animal move?

Distracted, silly or bored?
This way to feeling calm

Nervous, worried, embarrassed?
This way to feeling calm

Angry, cross, frustrated?
This way to feeling calm

Sad, lonely, unwell or tired?
This way to feeling calm

Message to Grown-ups

I am a primary school teacher and a certified STOTT PILATES® instructor. I have been working with children for over 20 years. My focus has always been the same – providing opportunities for all children to develop and improve their emotional and physical health.

This book is designed for parents, carers, teachers and professionals who want to support the physical and emotional wellbeing of their children through these motivating, fun exercises.

Read the book aloud, and do the moves together or on your own. Copy the animals breathing, bending and stretching and feel better on the inside as well as on the outside.

The exercises help physically to improve fine and gross motor skills, posture, alignment, flexibility, balance, coordination and core strength.

These exercises also improve wellbeing and, performed correctly, help children regulate their own emotions. The right sequence can change moods from distracted to focused. From frustrated to cooperative and from anxious to calm. Recognise how you are feeling and then choose the animal exercises to help.

These exercises can be done anywhere at any time with children of all ages, abilities and needs.

This book enables children to understand and manage their own emotions. After these exercises, children will be in a better place to listen, think and learn. They will also be able to talk, play, share and join in activities more productively.

I hope you enjoy Animals Move!

Printed in Great Britain
by Amazon

20685644R00025